W9-AHY-595

J
796.34
Bra
Bracken
Tennis

R537161
8.79

DATE DUE			
MY 2 7'92			
OC 19'93			

AN

GREAT RIVER REGIONAL LIBRARY
St. Cloud, Minnesota 56301

Be the Best
TENNIS

Play Like a Pro
By Charles Bracken

537161

Troll Associates

597 9042

Library of Congress Cataloging-in-Publication Data

Bracken, Charles.
   Tennis: play like a pro / by Charles Bracken.
     p.   cm.—(Be the best!)
   Summary: An introduction to the history and techniques of tennis
with advice on how to improve one's game.
   ISBN 0-8167-1931-4 (lib. bdg.) ISBN 0-8167-1932-2 (pbk.)
   1. Tennis—Juvenile literature. [1. Tennis.] I. Title.
II. Series.
GV996.5.B37 1990
796.342'2—dc20   89-27341

Copyright © 1990 by Troll Associates, Mahwah, New Jersey

All rights reserved. No part of this book may be used or reproduced in any manner whatsoever without written permission from the publisher.

Printed in the United States of America.

10 9 8 7 6 5 4 3 2 1

Be the Best

TENNIS

Play Like a Pro

FOREWORD

by Susan Patton

Tennis is a sport that can last a lifetime. People from ages four to ninety can be seen on tennis courts all over the world. It keeps you young, it keeps you fit, and it keeps you active.

Tennis, Play Like a Pro, will get you off to a sound start in the sport. Practice what you learn here with lots of your friends. You may even want to take a few lessons from a tennis pro or instructor. You can also read this fine book again after practicing awhile. You'll be surprised at how much more you'll learn by a second reading.

But first things first. Read this book through carefully. Then pick up a racket and some balls, head out to a court, and play one of the most exciting games any-where—tennis. Lots of luck!

Susan Patton

Susan Patton has been the head coach of women's tennis at Seton Hall University since 1973. Her teams have won an impressive 75 percent of the matches they've played, and team honors include a state championship. Since 1985, Susan has also been in charge of the men's tennis program at Seton Hall. As a player in her own right, Susan Patton has been both singles and doubles grass-court champion at Orange Lawn Tennis Club in New Jersey several times.

Contents

Tennis Is Terrific

Tennis is a racket game of speed, skill, and stamina. It is also a thinking athlete's sport. Tennis players do not just hit the ball back and forth over the net aimlessly. They use strategy and a variety of shots to prevent an opponent from returning the ball.

In many ways, tennis is a unique sport. Girls and boys can play tennis together and be evenly matched. Size is not much of a factor. Quick reflexes, agility, good timing, and endurance are what it takes to be a tennis player. But most of all, you have to be willing to learn and work hard.

Courtesy is also an important part of tennis. Fans watching a game are rarely loud or unruly. They usually applaud at the right time, not during play, so the concentration of the players won't be disturbed.

But polite as tennis may seem, it is fiercely competitive and often very exciting. A good tennis match has just as many thrills as any other major sporting event. That is what makes tennis so terrific! It is fun to learn, fun to play, and fun to watch.

The Story of Tennis

How and where did tennis begin? That question is not easy to answer. No one knows for sure just how or where tennis began. The ancient Egyptians, Greeks, and Persians all played games similar to tennis.

Several hundred years later, English and French nobility played an indoor game called royal or court tennis. It was played off four cement walls and over a sagging net. The game was something like a combination of tennis and jai alai (a game where players use a long, hand-shaped basket strapped to their wrist to propel the ball).

EGYPTIANS PLAYED TENNIS

The word *tennis* comes from the French word *tenetz*, meaning "take heed." "Tenetz" was shouted before the server in a tennis court game smashed the ball over the net to begin play.

At first, early royal tennis matches were played with just bare hands. Later, gloves and then a form of bat were used. Finally, strung rackets somewhat like the ones used today were introduced to the indoor game.

Tennis had existed in one form or another for many years before Major Walter Clopton Wingfield came onto the scene in the late 1800s. This English soldier is generally credited with inventing what would become the modern game of tennis.

At a party in Wales in 1873, Wingfield introduced a ball and racket game that he called *sphairistike*. It's a Greek word that means "playing ball." That name, however, was quickly replaced by *lawn tennis*.

Wingfield applied for a patent, which he received in

1874. He then began to package and sell lawn tennis nets and balls in England and other countries. Included with those nets and balls was a pamphlet he wrote on the rules of the game. There was also a diagram of an hourglass-shaped court, which was the official court at the time.

EARLY LAWN TENNIS

Soon, more and more people became interested in the sport of lawn tennis. And in 1875, a code of rules was published by the Marylebone Cricket Club in England.

The All-England Croquet and Lawn Tennis Club revised the rules in 1877 and became the governing body of the sport. That same year, the club sponsored the first major lawn tennis tournament ever held. It took place at the club's headquarters in Wimbledon, a London suburb. "Wimbledon" is the popular name for the All-England Championships.

Around 1877, lawn tennis began to look more and more like the modern game. The court was changed to its present rectangular shape. The net was improved and lowered, and the present-day system of scoring was also adopted.

Thanks to Mary Ewing Outerbridge of Staten Island, New York, tennis came to America in 1874. Outerbridge bought tennis equipment from British army officers in Bermuda and returned with it to the United States. The sport of tennis quickly caught on and became popular here.

In 1881, the first United States men's championship tournament was held at Newport, Rhode Island. In 1915, the United States Championships were moved to the West Side Tennis Club in Forest Hills, New York. And since 1978, the United States Championships, popularly called the U.S. Open, have been held at the National Tennis Center in Flushing Meadow, New York.

Besides the All-England and the United States championships, the French and the Australian championships are among the most important tournaments a player can win. In fact, winning all four of those championships in the same calendar year is called a *grand slam*. Don Budge in 1938 and Maureen Connolly in 1953 are the only two Americans ever to win a grand slam.

Over the years, tennis has become an international favorite among sports fans. And championship tournaments are now played in countries all over the globe.

What You Need
To Play Tennis

Tennis requires very little special equipment. All you need to play tennis are a racket, sneakers, a ball, and a playing court.

TENNIS RACKET

Tennis rackets usually have wood, graphite, or light metal frames. They are strung with gut or nylon. A racket weighs from eleven and a half to sixteen ounces and is usually about twenty-seven inches long. Players between the ages of nine and twelve should use a racket that

TENNIS RACKET

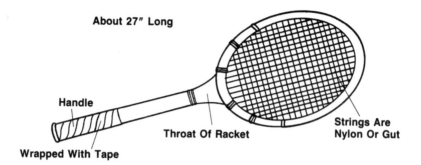

About 27" Long

Handle

Wrapped With Tape

Throat Of Racket

Strings Are
Nylon Or Gut

weighs between eleven and a half to twelve and a half ounces and has a handle size that measures four and a quarter to four and a half inches. Older players can use heavier rackets with thicker handles.

The size of a tennis racket handle varies. The proper handle size for you depends on the size of your hand. Your thumb should be able to reach the first joint of your middle finger when you grip the racket.

In picking a racket, select one that feels light and comfortable in your hand. It should also be well balanced. Never use a racket that feels even a little bit heavy at the hitting end. A heavy racket will tire your arm and make you lose control of the ball when you follow through on a stroke.

THE BALL

A standard tennis ball weighs about two ounces and is about two and a half inches in diameter. It is made of rubber, has a hollow center, and is coated with white or yellow cloth. Official tennis balls have to be approved by the U.S. Lawn Tennis Association.

CLOTHING

Tennis clothes do not have to be expensive. They should be simple, neat, and not restrict your movement. Shorts, loose shirts, white cotton socks, and sneakers are fine. There are also many kinds of tennis outfits for girls.

Official tournament play requires that players wear white clothing. The sneakers should also be white and light rather than heavy. Thick, white cotton socks are also best. They help absorb the impact of all the sudden stopping and turning you'll be doing on the tennis court. Avoid thin or normal dress socks. They can cause blisters.

TENNIS ATTIRE

White Shirt

Girl's One-Piece Tennis Outfit

White Shorts

White Socks And Sneakers

TENNIS COURT

A tennis court is built so that its ends face north and south. This helps players avoid the direct glare of the sun rising in the east or setting in the west.

A tennis court can be on grass or harder surfaces like special asphalt or clay. A regulation tennis court is seventy-eight feet long and thirty-six feet wide. It is divided in half by a net that is three feet high at the center and three and a half feet high at the posts that hold it up.

Lines are painted around the court to show its boundaries. Tennis courts have two sets of boundaries. The boundaries that are used depend on how many people are playing. In singles play (one person on each side of the net), the inside boundary lines are used. That means that the legal playing area is seventy-eight feet long and twenty-seven feet wide. In doubles play (two people on each side of the net), the outside lines form the legal playing area. They are seventy-eight feet long and thirty-six feet wide.

The back boundaries are *base lines.* The side boundaries are *sidelines.* The inside court lines that mark off the singles playing area are *tram lines,* or *singles sidelines.* The four-and-a-half foot distance between a *doubles sideline* and a tram line is the *alley.*

A tennis court also has other lines painted on it to show special areas. Each half of the court is divided by a line across it that is twenty-one feet from the net. That line is the *service line.*

TENNIS COURT

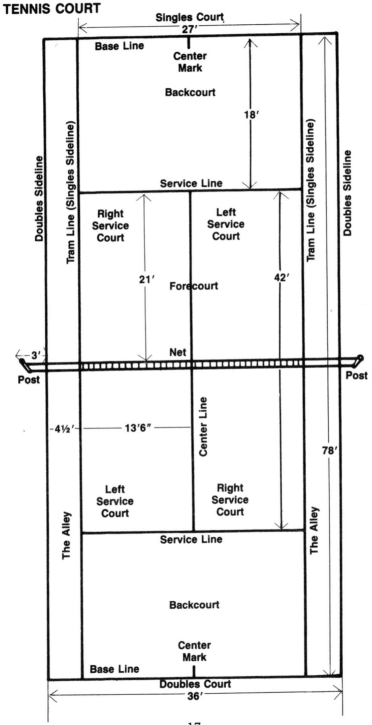

Singles Court
27'

Base Line

Center Mark

Backcourt

18'

Service Line

Right Service Court

Left Service Court

21'   Forecourt   42'

Net

Doubles Sideline

Tram Line (Singles Sideline)

Tram Line (Singles Sideline)

Doubles Sideline

←3'

Post   Post

-4½'   13'6"

Center Line

78'

Left Service Court

Right Service Court

The Alley

The Alley

Service Line

Backcourt

Center Mark

Base Line

Doubles Court
36'

17

The area behind the service line is called the *backcourt*. The backcourt measures eighteen feet from the service line to the base line. The area in front of the service line is called the *forecourt*. The forecourt is divided down the middle by the *center line*. As a player faces the net, the two halves created by the center line are known as the *left service court* and the *right service court*. Each service court area is thirteen feet six inches wide and twenty-one feet long from the net to the service line.

How to Score
And Play

Some people think tennis must be hard to learn. It's true that the sport requires a lot of work and a great deal of concentration. But the rules for scoring and playing a match are really not difficult to learn. And after a while, with continued practice and match play, they'll become second nature to you.

SCORING

A tennis match is made up of *sets* and *games*. To win a set, a player must win six games. In most cases, a player wins the match by winning two out of three sets. However, players must sometimes win three out of five sets to win a match.

A tennis game is won by scoring four points. In tennis, a score of zero is called *love*. The first point scored is called *fifteen*. The second point scored is called *thirty*, and the third point scored is called *forty*. The fourth and final point scored is called *game*, meaning that the game is over.

If the score is tied at three points each, that is called *deuce*. When the score is at deuce, a player must score two points in a row to win the game. In tennis, the margin of victory must always be at least two points.

If the score is at deuce and a player scores one point, that player is said to have the *advantage*, or "ad." If that player scores the next point, he or she wins the game. If the opposing player scores a point instead, the score returns to deuce. Then the game continues until one of the players scores two points in a row.

PLAYING

Tennis can be played by two or four people at one time. If two people play (one on each side of the net), it is called a *singles match*. If four people play (two partners on each side of the net), it is called a *doubles match*. A *mixed doubles match* features two teams, each made up of a girl and a boy.

To start a singles match, one person must serve. Usually players toss a coin or in some other way decide who will have *service*. Service is hitting the ball first to start the match. The winner of the coin toss wins the right to serve. The loser gets to pick a side of the net.

TENNIS PLAY BEGINS ①
WITH A SERVE

If the winner of the toss wants to choose a side of the net instead, the loser gets to serve. However, it usually is best to serve if you win the toss. In many cases, serving gives a player a big advantage. Returning a good serve can be very tough.

To start the match, the server stands behind the base line (see page 16). His or her feet should be to the right of the *center mark* (the short hash mark in the middle of the base line) and to the left of the tram line. Then the server throws the ball up and hits it over the net diagonally into the opponent's right service court. (See pages 45-47 for more on the service stroke.)

The player receiving the serve must let the ball bounce once before returning it. After the serve, the ball can be hit to any part of the court and no longer has to bounce once before it can be legally returned. The ball can even be hit in the air before it bounces, 'which is an advantage at times.

The ball must land within the boundaries of the court at all times. If the ball hits outside the base line or sidelines, it is called *out.* The player who hits the ball out loses the point to his or her opponent.

THAT SHOT IS NO GOOD... IT'S OUT!

Sideline

After a point is scored, the server goes to the other side of the center mark on the base line and begins play again with another serve. The server moves from one side to the other after each point is made. And the same person serves until the game is over. Then the other person gets to serve in the next game. After that, the players take turns serving after each game throughout the match. And opposing players switch sides on the court after the first, third, and every subsequent odd-numbered game played.

A served ball that lands out or doesn't get over the net is called a *fault*. After one fault, you are allowed a second serve. However, if your second serve is also no good, you *double fault*. That means your opponent automatically wins the point.

If your serve hits the net and then goes over it into the correct service court of your opponent, a *let* is called. That means your serve is no good. But it also means you can take the serve over without being called for a fault or losing the point. There is no limit to the number of lets that can be called on a serve.

When you serve, you are not allowed to step on or over the base line until you hit the ball. If you do step on the base line before hitting the ball on a serve, you commit a *foot fault*. It's treated just like a regular fault. In other words, a foot fault on your first serve makes it no good. You must now go to your second serve. And if you commit a foot fault on your second serve, you lose the point.

FOOT FAULT EXAMPLE

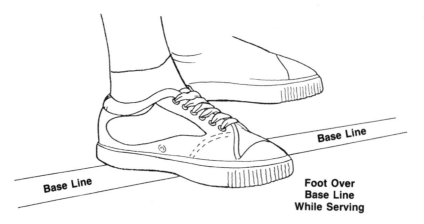

Base Line

Base Line

Foot Over
Base Line
While Serving

In tennis, you can lose a point in progress several different ways. If you don't return the ball over the net, you lose the point. If you hit a ball outside your opponent's court, you lose the point. If you fail to hit a ball *before* it bounces twice, you lose the point. Lastly, if you hit a ball more than once with your racket, you lose the point.

Unlike some other sporting events, tennis matches do not have time limits. Play continues until the match is won, no matter how long it may take. And the margin of victory must always be at least two points.

DOUBLES PLAY

In doubles play, there are two players on each team. Those team players must work well together. Two great singles players do not always make a great doubles team. Cooperation and teamwork are the keys to a good doubles pair.

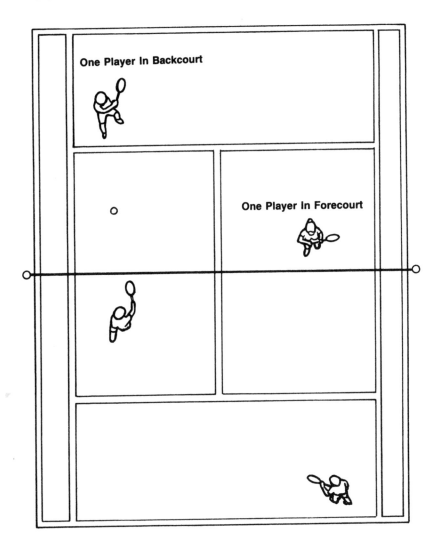

The size of the court for doubles play is wider than for singles play (see page 16). This gives doubles players a bit more room to operate. Usually, beginners position themselves so one player is in the forecourt near the net and one player is in the backcourt. They also try to stay on opposite sides of the center line.

However, depending on their opponents' shots during a game, players on a doubles team may switch front and back positions and occasionally even switch sides of the court.

For doubles play, the teams are set up so a player on one side of the net in the forecourt is opposite an opponent positioned in the backcourt.

As skill level improves, a backcourt player can approach the net, next to his or her partner, and volley away shots for winners.

Gripping the Racket

Make sure you have a racket that feels comfortable in your hand (see page 13). Once you do, you can then learn the standard ways of gripping the handle for the forehand, backhand, and service strokes.

The first two grips discussed here are forehand grips. That means you'll be hitting the ball by moving the palm or front of your hand forward toward the net.

EASTERN FOREHAND GRIP

An easy way to learn how to hold a racket correctly for a forehand stroke is to place the racket on a flat surface like a desk or table. Now balance the racket on its edge so the strings are not face down on the flat surface.

With the hand you *won't* use for swinging the racket, lift the racket off the table by holding it up near the racket head. Keep it at the same angle as it was on the table. With your other hand, reach out as if to shake hands with the handle. Grip the handle at the bottom, holding it firmly but not too tightly. You can now drop away your opposite hand from just below the racket head.

FOREHAND GRIP

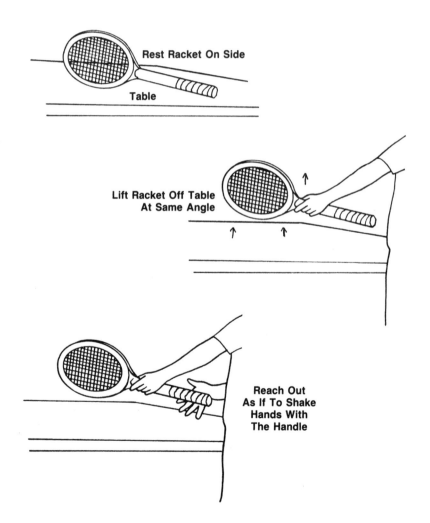

Rest Racket On Side

Table

Lift Racket Off Table At Same Angle

Reach Out As If To Shake Hands With The Handle

Keep your fingers together. Your forefinger should reach around the handle to the first joint of your next finger. Your thumb should wrap around the handle from the opposite side and press against the end of your forefinger. That will give your stroke firmness and added strength against the impact of the ball.

EASTERN FOREHAND GRIP

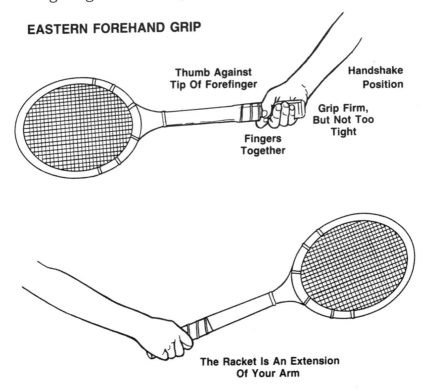

Thumb Against
Tip Of Forefinger

Handshake
Position

Grip Firm,
But Not Too
Tight

Fingers
Together

The Racket Is An Extension
Of Your Arm

In the eastern forehand grip and in all grips, the position of your forearm and wrist is important. It's as if the racket were an extension of your arm. The wrist must be kept firm to prevent the racket from wobbling when the ball is hit. When striking the ball, make sure the face of the racket hits flat against it.

The eastern forehand grip reduces strain on the arm and provides a natural, easy swing. It also adds to the swiftness with which the ball bounces off the court. In tennis, that is called *pace*. In addition, the eastern forehand grip increases the speed of the ball in the air.

Another advantage to this grip is that it allows players to hit high or low shots equally well. The eastern forehand grip can be used for the forehand drive (see page 39), the volley (see page 49), or the lob (see page 51).

WESTERN FOREHAND GRIP

This grip got its name from the place where it originated: the western coast of the United States. It was developed for use on asphalt courts where the ball takes higher bounces than on eastern grass courts.

WESTERN FOREHAND GRIP

Palm Faces Up
Toward The Sky

The western forehand grip is not really a good one for beginners. It can put strain on the arm when hitting low shots, and it can be awkward and difficult to use.

In the western forehand grip, the handle is gripped with the palm facing up toward the sky (see diagram) rather than in the handshake position of the eastern forehand grip. The position of the fingers, however, is exactly the same as in the eastern forehand grip (see pages 27-29).

The basic problem with the western forehand grip is that it is *very* difficult to keep the face of the racket level with the ball on shots waist-high or lower.

BACKHAND GRIP

The backhand grip is basically the eastern forehand grip with some minor variations. The changes are necessary because in a backhand stroke the ball is struck with the side of the racket opposite the one used in the forehand stroke.

BACKHAND GRIP

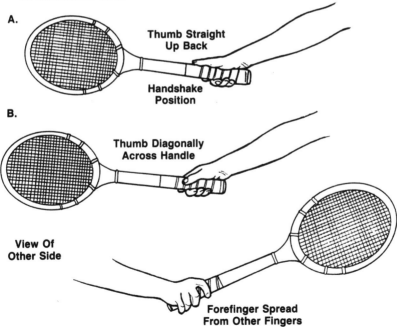

A.

Thumb Straight
Up Back

Handshake
Position

B.

Thumb Diagonally
Across Handle

View Of
Other Side

Forefinger Spread
From Other Fingers

To begin with, the position of the thumb in the backhand grip differs from that in the forehand grip. In most cases, it is best *not* to wrap your thumb around the handle for this grip. Wrapping your thumb around the handle puts extra strain on your wrist when you hit the ball.

Some players using the backhand grip place the thumb diagonally across the back of the handle for support. Doing that also adds firmness to the stroke. However, sometimes this positioning of the thumb makes it a bit more difficult to meet the ball squarely. Still, this thumb position is popular with many players who have a strong backhand.

Other players using the backhand grip put the thumb straight up the back of the handle. Placing the thumb straight up the back makes it easier to keep the racket face flat and steady when striking the ball. This thumb position is best for beginners.

Depending on the shot they want to make, advanced players often switch the position of the thumb on the racket during a game. For one shot, the thumb may be diagonally across the handle. But on another shot, the thumb may be straight up the back. After mastering the backhand stroke, you may want to experiment in this way.

Another difference in the backhand grip is that the forefinger, or index finger, is spread from the other three. You'll remember that in the eastern forehand grip (see page 29), the fingers are pressed together. That is not the case here. The other fingers are also on a slight angle, with the heel of the hand resting against the butt of the handle. Placing the hand there helps prevent the racket from slipping out of your hand during the stroke.

SERVICE GRIP

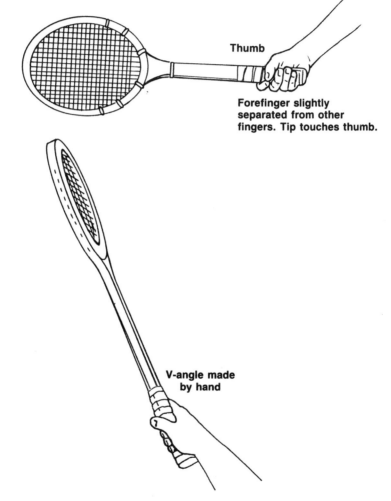

Thumb

Forefinger slightly
separated from other
fingers. Tip touches thumb.

V-angle made
by hand

SERVICE GRIP

Service is when you put the ball in play to start a game. It also has a standard grip for beginners, sort of a halfway grip between a forehand and backhand grip.

The basic service grip is sometimes called the continental grip because it was first developed in Europe. The continental grip is like the eastern forehand grip in the way the racket is held. Your thumb should be down across the front surface of the handle and should touch the *tip* of the forefinger. Your forefinger should be slightly separated from the other fingers, which are pressed together. The tip of your forefinger should not be wrapped as far around the handle as in the eastern forehand grip.

More about the mechanics of service will be discussed later in Chapter 7, "Basic Tennis Strokes."

THE SERVE

Good Tennis
Technique

You now know how to grip a racket. And the tennis strokes discussed in the next chapter will show you how to use it. But before going any further, you should learn about good tennis technique. That includes:

HITTING THE BALL

Concentration, good form, and follow-through are important to hitting a tennis ball well. Concentration is simply paying attention to the game and keeping your eyes on the ball at all times. Your eyes should be on the ball even as the racket strikes it. Never look away or turn your head. Always watch the ball.

You'll learn about good form in the following chapter, which explains the basic strokes of tennis. That's where you'll learn how to position your body for different shots.

FOLLOW-THROUGH

**Racket Continues In
Direction Of Swing**

Follow-through is allowing your racket to continue in the direction of your swing to a certain degree even after you strike the ball. Following through will increase the speed and accuracy of your shots.

CONDITIONING

Some people think you do not have to be physically fit to play tennis. That just isn't so. Tennis is a physically demanding game, and tennis players have to be in excellent physical condition. Players must dash all over the court to return shots.

CONDITIONING

It takes lots of endurance to play tennis. Remember, there is no time limit on a tennis match. Sometimes a hotly contested match may last for hours. So if you want to be a good tennis player, make sure you are in shape before you step out on the court.

FOOTWORK

When you're hitting the tennis ball, the position of your feet is very important. It can determine the direction of your stroke. When using a forehand stroke, try to face the right sideline and keep your left foot closest to the net. When using a backhand stroke, face the left sideline and keep your right foot closest to the net. (Reverse the position of your feet if you're left-handed.) At all times, stay up on the balls of your feet. Never play flat-footed with your heels down.

Basic Tennis Strokes

There are several basic strokes in tennis. In this section, you will learn all about them.

FOREHAND DRIVE

The forehand drive is the main stroke in tennis. To play competitively, you must master the forehand drive. It makes the ball travel on a low-level line rather than on a high arc.

To start, use the eastern forehand grip (see page 27). Stand in a good ready position on the balls of your feet. Crouch slightly.

Do not let your free arm just dangle at your side. In tennis, the free arm is used in two ways. First, it's used to counterbalance the arm holding the racket during a stroke. Second, while you're waiting to hit the ball, your free hand helps support the weight of the racket.

Now stand slightly facing the right sideline. Support the racket by placing your free hand lightly on the top, or *throat*, of the handle. That is the part of the handle nearest the head. Remember, only hold it lightly between your fingertips. After a shot, return the racket to this support position.

Always make sure the face of your racket is toward the net. Never hold it face up like a frying pan. Keep the handle out away from your body, holding the racket about waist high. It should be positioned in the middle of your body, not to one side.

**READY POSITION FOR
FOREHAND DRIVE**

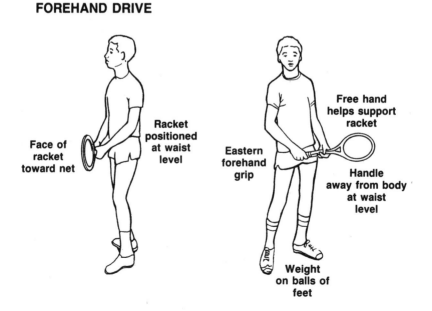

Face of racket toward net

Racket positioned at waist level

Eastern forehand grip

Free hand helps support racket

Handle away from body at waist level

Weight on balls of feet

As the ball approaches, keep your eyes on it and go to it. Do not wait for the ball to come to you. If you're right-handed, position your body to the left of the ball's line of flight. (Reverse this body position if you're left-handed.) You should end up facing the right sideline, with your left foot closer to the net than your right foot. (Again, the reverse is true for left-handed players.) Your body and shoulders should be parallel to the flight of the ball.

Now swing your racket backward first before moving forward. That is called the *back swing*. Make sure your body is well away from the ball so you do not hinder your own swing.

During the back swing, keep your elbow bent and low. Hold the racket at almost a right angle to your forearm. Halfway through the back swing, release your support hand. Swing the racket back behind your body and then forward. Pause only very briefly between the two motions.

Bring your racket forward in a straight line with the ball. Keep your eyes on the ball and time your swing. You want your racket to strike the ball just a little in front of your body.

As you swing, shift your weight to your front foot. Use your left arm as a counterbalance. Do not try to hit the ball too hard. Concentrate on making the ball go where you want it to go, keeping your wrist firm.

During your swing, turn your body to the left to add force and accuracy to your stroke. (Turn your body to the right if you're left-handed.) It is just like getting

FOREHAND DRIVE

1. Keep elbow bent and arm low. Position body to left of ball.

2. Pause briefly, then swing racket forward to hit ball.

3. Follow through. Keep your eyes on the ball.

your body into a swing in baseball. The racket should meet the ball flat. That means the face of the racket is held straight up, not tilted up or down.

After hitting the ball, follow through. Allow your racket to continue moving forward. It should end up at about eye level, pointing in the direction the ball has gone.

A ball that bounces is called a *ground stroke.* It is best to hit a ground stroke when it is waist-high. If possible, never bend at the waist to hit a shot below the waist. Instead, bend at the knees. Bending over at the waist will put you off balance.

To hit a forehand drive to the left, put your front foot slightly to the left and do not use a lot of back swing. Meet the ball in front of your left hip. This will help get your body into the shot.

To hit down the middle, step straight into the ball and strike it directly in front of your stomach.

To hit to the right, step right and use more back swing. Also, meet the ball deeper at your right hip.

BACKHAND STROKE

If a ball is hit to your backhand side, *never* try to run around the ball to hit it with a forehand drive. Trying to do that will not only place you in an awkward position, but it will also leave too much of the court uncovered. Learn to use a backhand stroke as readily as a forehand drive. You cannot be a complete tennis player without a good backhand.

Begin by holding the handle with the backhand grip (see page 31). The way to hit a backhand drive is the same as a forehand drive—but done in reverse.

The mechanics of the backhand stroke will be described from the standpoint of a right-handed player here. Once again, your left hand helps hold the racket while you're waiting for the ball. The fingertips of your left hand should grip the racket lightly at the throat.

BACKHAND STROKE

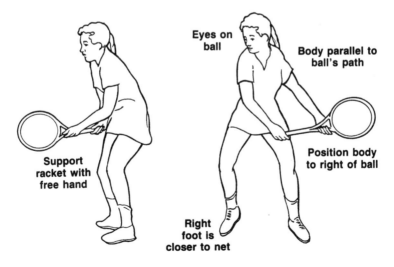

Support racket with free hand

Eyes on ball

Body parallel to ball's path

Position body to right of ball

Right foot is closer to net

43

As the ball approaches, position yourself to the right of the ball's path. Face the left sideline and keep your right foot closer to the net. The ball is played to your left side. As in the forehand drive, your body should be parallel to the ball's path. Your right shoulder should be turned to the net from the time you begin your back swing until the time you complete the stroke. If you do not keep your shoulder in that position throughout the stroke, you will lose power and accuracy and end up off balance.

During the back swing of a backhand stroke, keep your support fingers on the racket until halfway through the forward swing. (You will recall that in a forehand drive, the support fingers slip off during the back swing.)

BACKHAND

A. Waiting

B. Position yourself to right

C. Support hand *stays on* during back swing

D. Support hand stays on until halfway through forward swing / Shift weight back

E. Wrist firm, elbow bent

F. Straighten arm after ball is hit / Follow through

SERVICE STROKE

The service stroke is the most powerful of all tennis strokes. However, it is important to remember not to try to kill the first ball on a serve. Accuracy is more important than power. A ball that is served out is a fault. A server who has two faults in a row double faults and loses the point to his or her opponent (see page 23). So always try to make your first serve good.

Serving the ball gives a player a great advantage. If done effectively, serves are almost always difficult to return. A good serve that is not returned gives the server a point and is called an *ace.*

SERVE POSITION

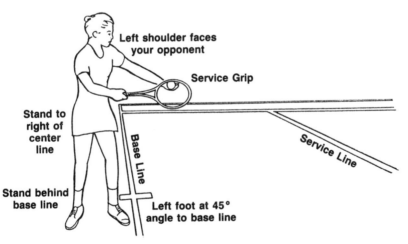

To serve, use the continental grip (see page 34). Near the middle of the court, stand to the right of the center mark and a few inches behind the base line. Face the right side of the court, with your left foot placed at an angle of forty-five degrees to the base line. Your left shoulder should face your opponent.

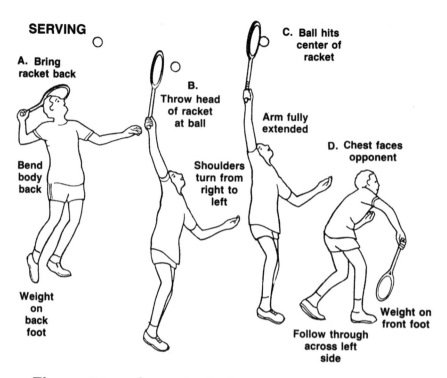

SERVING

A. Bring racket back

Bend body back

Weight on back foot

B. Throw head of racket at ball

Shoulders turn from right to left

C. Ball hits center of racket

Arm fully extended

D. Chest faces opponent

Follow through across left side

Weight on front foot

The position of your body is very important in the serve. Good body position increases the power and accuracy of your shot and will give you better balance during your stroke.

To begin, lower your right shoulder and bend your body way back. Shift almost all your weight to your back foot. Now toss the ball four or five feet into the air above you. Your toss should send the ball a bit forward and to the side so it is in a position above your left toe. Keep your eyes on the ball during the toss.

A serve is an overhand stroke. The racket is brought way back behind your body for the back swing. The arm comes up from the back swing just as if the head of the racket was being thrown at the ball. The racket face is straightened as it goes to the ball. The ball should hit the center of the racket strings when the arm and racket are fully extended. Remember, the racket comes forward in an overhand motion over the top of the shoulder.

As your racket comes toward the ball, your shoulders should turn from right to left. That way, when the ball is hit, your chest will be facing your opponent. Your body weight should also shift from your back foot to your front foot as your racket comes forward. All your weight should end up on your front foot as you follow through. The follow-through should be across your left side.

Remember, make a good toss when serving. And always keep your eyes on the ball. Try to make your first serve good to avoid the possibility of a double fault. Do not foot fault (see page 23). After both your feet come to a rest prior to a serve, it is a fault if you change their position. So don't walk, run, leap into the air, or step on or across the base line before the ball is hit.

THE SMASH

A forehand smash is just like a serve. The big difference is you do not toss the ball up for yourself. In a way, it is your opponent who tosses the ball up for you. That is usually done in the form of a high, soft shot known as a *lob* (see page 51).

Like the serve, the smash is an overhand stroke. It is usually hit between the service line and the net. The smash is hit downward in such a powerful fashion that the ball quickly bounces beyond the opponent's reach.

To hit a smash, draw your racket far back behind your head. Watch the ball closely. More so than in any other stroke, your eyes must be on the ball to hit a smash effectively.

To meet the ball, raise yourself up onto your toes to get maximum height for the smash. You want to hit the ball downward. Sometimes you might even have to jump into the air to reach a lob. As your racket swings forward to meet the ball, your arm should straighten and your weight should shift forward. You may only be able to get your upper body into the swing if you have to jump in the air for a smash. Still, follow through by bringing the racket down across your body.

FOREHAND SMASH

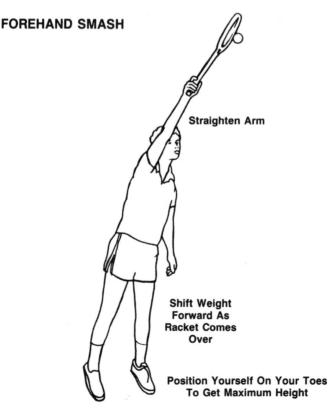

Straighten Arm

Shift Weight
Forward As
Racket Comes
Over

Position Yourself On Your Toes
To Get Maximum Height

THE VOLLEY

Ball Is Hit Before It Bounces

Short Back Swing

Feet Spread

VOLLEY

A volley is a return shot made before the ball hits your side of the court. In a volley, you hit the ball in the air before it can bounce. A volley is used when a player is going to the net or is positioned close to the net.

The grips used for a volley are the same ones used for the forehand drive or the backhand stroke. The body and feet are in the same position as for a forehand drive (see page 39) or a backhand stroke (see page 43), depending on which side the ball is hit. However, a volley is more difficult because you normally don't have time to plant your feet correctly. When hitting a volley, keep your feet spread and play on the balls of your feet. To get your body into the stroke, shift your weight to the foot nearest the ball on the swing.

One of the secrets to a successful volley is the back swing. Your back swing should be very short. Keep the head of your racket higher than your wrist, and punch at the ball rather than swing at it. Make sure you meet the ball with the racket face flat if the ball is above the net. If it is below the net, keep the face of your racket slightly open or facing upward. Also, keep your wrist securely locked. The follow-through in the volley is very short.

When hitting a volley, try to keep the ball down and win the point on that one stroke. Otherwise, if your volley does not win the point, you may find yourself out of position and unable to return the next shot.

HALF-VOLLEY

The half-volley, or trap, is mainly used to return a difficult shot that bounces at your feet. The ball is stroked just after it hits the court—sort of like a short hop in baseball. For a half-volley, your body should be turned sideways as it would during regular strokes. But there is almost no back swing to a half-volley. Hold your racket firmly and bring the head up slightly on the swing to put *top spin* (see page 57) on the ball. There is no follow-through.

When using the half-volley, a right-handed player should have his or her weight shifted to the left foot for a forehand stroke and to the right foot for a back-hand stroke.

HALF-VOLLEY

**Use half-volley
on ball that bounces
at your feet**

LOB

A lob is a softly hit stroke that lifts the ball high in the air over the head of an opponent at the net. It is usually made from the backcourt.

To hit a lob, hold the racket by using the same grip as you would for regular ground strokes. Do not try to use a shortened swing. To be successful, you must try to disguise the lob. Otherwise, your opponent will recover too quickly and get into easy position to return your lob with a smash (see page 47).

Hit the ball upward, holding your wrist loosely. The face of your racket must be open or facing upward. The swing comes from underneath the ball and up. Using a slow motion, try to hit the ball right in the middle of the racket. It is usually best to lob over an opponent's backhand side because the shot will be harder to return from there.

THE LOB

Hit Ball Upward

Racket Faces Up

YIPES!

Loose Wrist

Frequently, a lob is made off a volley return and is called a *lob volley.* It is meant to surprise and catch an opponent off guard. A lob volley is used for one of two reasons. It can be a defensive shot, giving you time to get back into good position. It can also be an offensive shot used against an opponent who is caught up near the net.

DROP SHOT

A drop shot is used when your opponent is at the back part of the court. It is a stroke hit just hard enough to clear the net and then land dead on the other side with very little bounce. To hit a drop shot, you should be very close to the net. In fact, you should be close enough actually to reach out and touch the net. Under

THE DROP SHOT

no circumstances, however, should you or your racket touch the net. If you do, you will lose the point to your opponent.

Hit the drop shot by allowing the ball to just graze against the racket strings. It is a very soft shot without much swing. In fact, there is no back swing or follow-through.

CHOP STROKE

The chop is a stroke used mostly from the base line. It is one of the oldest known tennis strokes. Chopping the ball will cause it to bounce weakly almost straight up in the air.

THE CHOP

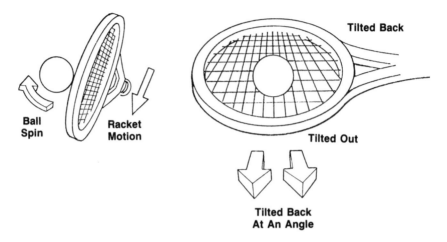

Ball Spin Racket Motion Tilted Back Tilted Out

Tilted Back
At An Angle

Chopping a ball puts a special spin on it. To get that spin, hold the face of your racket at a slight angle so that the top of your racket leans back toward you and the bottom leans out away from you. Hold your racket at about a fifteen-degree slant.

Swing the racket downward. The face should go down across the surface of the ball. It is like a chopping motion, which is how the stroke got its name. There is no follow-through on a chop stroke. The racket is brought to a quick stop after the ball is hit.

FLAT DRIVE

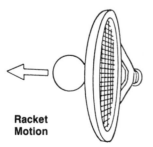

Racket Motion

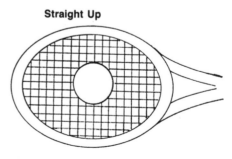

Straight Up

Straight Down

Putting Spin
On the Ball

Another important part of the game of tennis is putting spin on the ball. Generally, you learned how to hit the ball flat during a stroke. In this flat drive, the racket is held straight up and down facing the net. A ball that is hit flat usually goes straight and has just a slight spin.

Holding the face of your racket at different angles, however, can make your serves and strokes harder to return. By using these different angles, you can make the ball swerve right or left or cause it to bounce in a tricky way.

My head's spinning!

To help you understand how to put spin on the ball, think of the ball as having a top, a bottom, a front, and a back. The back is the part of the ball nearest your racket.

SLICE

A slice puts backspin on the ball. (Backspin is a ball rotating in the air *toward* the person who hit it and *away* from the person who'll receive it.) This causes the ball either to "sit up" on the court or to break right or left of an opponent.

To do a slice serve, swing your racket down across the side of the ball with a swift motion of the racket face.

In a slice, the racket is held on an angle (as in the chop stroke) during contact with the ball. The angle is greater than in the chop stroke, however. The top of the racket

THE SLICE

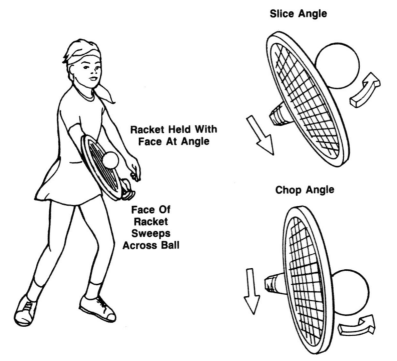

Slice Angle

Racket Held With
Face At Angle

Chop Angle

Face Of
Racket
Sweeps
Across Ball

should be tilted back more toward the player. Sweep the racket face across the back of the ball. It is almost like the angle of a knife used to slice a Thanksgiving turkey. But unlike the chop stroke, the slice requires a follow-through.

TOP SPIN

Top spin is a ball rotating *away* from the person who hit it and *toward* the person who'll receive it. It will cause the ball to skip quickly off the surface of the court and break wide and high to the right or left of an opponent. Top-spin serves are often very effective.

ANGLE OF RACKET FOR TOP SPIN

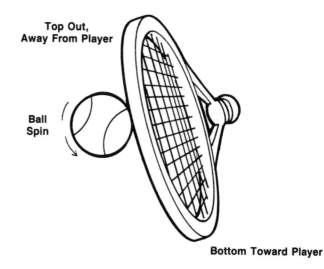

Top Out, Away From Player

Ball Spin

Bottom Toward Player

To add top spin to the ball, move your racket face from the back and up over the top of the ball. The angle of the racket as it hits the ball is much different from that in the chop stroke or slice. Angle the top of the racket away from you while keeping the bottom of the racket closer to you. That will cause the ball to spin with a rapidly downward motion.

When the ball strikes the court, it will bounce up very high.

Tennis Tips

You've just hit a great stroke. Now what do you do? Never stand around and watch the ball after you make a shot in tennis. While you're patting yourself on the back, your opponent may return the ball and catch you off guard and out of position. After you make a shot, always get ready for a return shot from your opponent.

In tennis, a player should always try to take a ball from a position near the net or at the base line. Getting caught between those two points, in an area sometimes called "no man's land," will make returning the ball very difficult for you. Another place where you *don't* want to be caught dawdling is near the sidelines.

The general rule of thumb in tennis is to get to a "safe" position on the court after your stroke. Usually that "safe" position is either right in front of the net or near the base line. If you want to hit your next stroke from the base line, get to a spot about a yard behind the middle of it. If you want to hit your next shot at the net, get to a position two or three yards back from the middle of it.

Keep in mind, however, that playing at the net is usually riskier than playing at the base line. An opponent can more easily hit the ball past or over you if you're standing at the net.

COURT "SAFE" POSITIONS

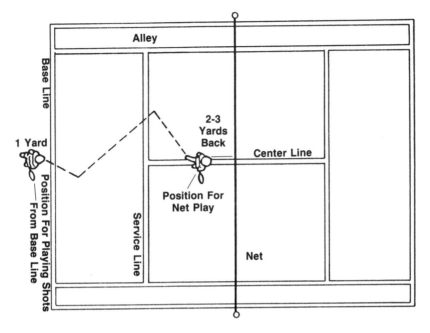

DOUBLES POSITIONS

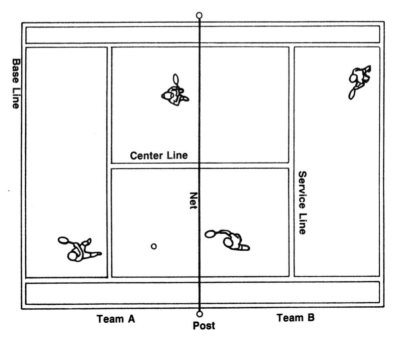

Missing The Ball On The Serve Is A Fault

No Surprise Serves

Another tip a beginner should keep in mind is that a server is not allowed to serve until the receiver is ready. "Surprise" serves are not allowed in tennis. And if a server tosses a ball up, swings at it, and misses, that counts as a fault.

Finally, if the ball you hit during play strikes the net, posts, metal cable, or cord and lands inbounds on your opponent's court, your shot is good.

Practice

Practicing your tennis strokes on a court with a friend can be helpful and fun. Remember that it is practice, *not* a match. Don't try to kill the ball or get too fancy. The idea is to work on your game, stroke by stroke. Pay attention to your form throughout.

If you can't find someone to practice with, you can still practice alone. A good way to practice your strokes is to hit a tennis ball against a high wall in a school yard or playground. You can also bring a bucket of tennis balls with you to a court where you can practice your serve. Concentrate more on accuracy than power at first.

Tennis is a great sport. It can be played on indoor or outdoor courts and can provide hours of fun exercise. So now that you know the basics of how to play it, go out and enjoy it. See you on the court!

INDEX